STOCK MARKET INVESTING FOR BEGINNERS

Learn how to Trade for a Living with Risk-Management Strategies. Invest in Options and Forex with "Trader-Psychology" techniques. Get your own Financial Freedom

MARK BROKER

© Copyright 2020 - All rights reserved.

The content contained within this book may not be reproduced, duplicated or transmitted without direct written permission from the author or the publisher.

Under no circumstances will any blame or legal responsibility be held against the publisher, or author, for any damages, reparation, or monetary loss due to the information contained within this book. Either directly or indirectly.

Legal Notice:

This book is copyright protected. This book is only for personal use. You cannot amend, distribute, sell, use, quote or paraphrase any part, or the content within this book, without the consent of the author or publisher.

Disclaimer Notice:

Please note the information contained within this document is for educational and entertainment purposes only. All effort has been executed to present accurate, up to date, and reliable, complete information. No warranties of any kind are declared or implied. Readers acknowledge that the author is not engaging in the rendering of legal, financial, medical or professional advice. The content within this book has been derived from various sources. Please consult a licensed professional before attempting any techniques outlined in this book.

By reading this document, the reader agrees that under no circumstances is the author responsible for any losses, direct or indirect, which are incurred as a result of the use of information contained within this document, including, but not limited to, — errors, omissions, or inaccuracies.

TABLE OF CONTENT

INTRODUCTION 1
1. THE ABC OF STOCK MARKET 3
What Is The Stock Market? 4
Who Integrates It? 4
Role of the Stock Exchange 5
How Does The Stock Market Work? 5
Can I Invest In The Stock Market From Home? 7
Invest in the stock market: What platform to use? 8
How much money do I have to invest in the stock market? 9
Can I start investing in a stock simulator? 10
2. THE MECHANICS OF OWNING, BUYING AND SELLING STOCKS 11
Buy Shares to Become A Shareholder 11
    Buy and sell stocks with online brokers 12
    Purchase and sale orders for shares 13
When is it the best time to buy shares on the stock exchange? ... 13
    When is it a good idea to sell the shares on the stock exchange? 14
    How long do you have to hold stocks in a short-term strategy? . 15
    How long do you have to keep stocks in a long-term strategy? .. 16
    When should the shares be resold? 16
    What shares can be purchased or sold online? 17
    What stocks to invest in? 17
3. WHO IS A BROKER & HOW TO CHOOSE ONE 19
Stockbroker: What is it? 19
    Stockbroker: Functions 20
    Characteristics of a Stockbroker 20
    How to choose the right stockbroker? 21
A Background Check Is a Must 21
    Interviewing multiple runners is a must. 22
    Check out these red flags. 23
    Do your homework with references. 24

4. HOW TO ASSESS RISK AND VOLATILITY 25

    Individual risk assessment 25

    Systematic risk assessment 26

    Standard Deviation 27

    Beta27 27

    Value at risk 27

    Conditional Value at risk 27

  What is Volatility? 28

    Implied Volatility 30

    Historical Volatility 31

5. TOP INDICATORS OF A WINNING INVESTMENT 33

    Trend line 33

    Simple Moving Average 34

    Rate of change 35

    Relative strength Index 36

    Moving Average Convergence Divergence 37

    Bollinger Bands 38

    Fibonacci Retracements 39

    All about Technical Indicators 40

6. BASIC INVESTMENT TECHNIQUES 44

  10 Basic Investment Techniques for Beginners 45

7. WHAT YOU SHOULD KNOW ABOUT TAXES 52

    The Long-term Capital Gains Rate Criteria 53

    Reducing Tax on your Stock Sales 53

    Experimenting with the Wash Rule 55

    Deduction of Capital Losses 56

    Other Deductible Expenses in Investment 56

    Final verdict 57

8. ALL ABOUT THE BULL & BEAR MARKET 59

    High Gross Domestic Products 60

    Rising Stock Prices 61

    Longer Stock Trading 61

    Lower Unemployment Rates 61

The Bull Market History 61
The Bear Market Indicators 63
The Bear Market History 64

9. COMMON STOCK EXCHANGE TERMS AND WHAT THEY MEAN 66

What is the Stock Market? 66
   1- Annual Report 67
   2- Arbitrage 67
   3- Averaging Down 67
   4- Bear Market 68
   5- Bull Market 68
   6- Beta 68
   7- Blue Chip Stocks 68
   8- Bourse 69
   9- Broker 69
   10- Bid 69
   11- Close 69
   12- Day trading 70
   13- Dividend 70
   14- Exchange 70
   15- Execution 70
   16- Haircut 71
   17- High 71
   18- Initial Public Offering 71
   19- Leverage 71
   20- Low 72
   21- Margin 72
   22- Moving Average 72
   23- Open 72
   24- Order 73
   25- pink sheet stocks 73
   26- Sector 73

10. TIPS AND TRICKS FOR INVESTING IN THE STOCK EXCHANGE 74
    1- Invest in Index Fund 74
    2- Focus on Mutual Funds 75
    3- Timing the Market 75
    4- Set Goals 75
    5- Five Golden steps of trading to learn: 76
    6- Have a balance of investments 76
    7- Think for long term 77
    8- Buy value stocks 77
    9- Diversify investments among sectors 77
    10- How much risk you can take? 78
    11- Control your emotions 78
    12- 360 Degree View 78
    13- Automate stocks 79
    14- Say no to leverage 79
    15- Choose one sector 79
    16- Risk vs. Return 79
    17- Buy low sell higher 80
    Final Word 80
CONCLUSION 82

INTRODUCTION

D id you know how many companies are registered with NYSE (New York Stock Exchange) and how much has been invested overall?

Here is a rough estimate: According to recent data, more than 3,000 companies have been registered, while the overall investment in just one stock exchange (NYSE) is about $15 Trillian.

Think of the other stock exchanges…..

The value of the international stock exchange is said to be $80 Trillian, Big Money – yeah – that means bigger gains…if you are in the game and (can play it correctly).

Now the question is how to learn it? Simple, follow the guidelines given in this comprehensive book, and you will be ready to play.

What's more interesting is 52 percent of Americans are Stock exchange investors. That shows how lucrative this market is.

So, before you start investing, read to learn the ABC of the stock market. It is written after doing research and is reviewed by some of the most successful investors.

Hope you would like this effort and enjoy reading and applying the strategies given in this book. In the end, if you ask me what that one thing that I should tell you as an expert to keep in mind (before beginning) is – it is: always remember: "a good Investment is always boring!"

> *"If investing is entertaining, if you're having fun, you're probably not making any money. Good investing is boring."*
>
> – George Soros

1. THE ABC OF STOCK MARKET

When we talk about investing in the stock market, we must understand that it is more than buying and selling shares. This activity can also be linked to other financial instruments where it is possible to operate in the short, medium, or long term.

The investment method used in the stock market is called "invest" if it is long term or "trading" if it is short.

Stock trading has become popular in this area of the stock market. This activity can be started online from anywhere in the world and consists of the sale and purchase of financial assets.

Trading consists of buying or selling an asset, then reselling or repurchasing it, and obtaining the respective profit. The advent of online trading has allowed many to invest in the stock market with little money, without owning large amounts of capital.

To manage the stock market, it is important to document yourself and study well the type of investment you are going to make.

What Is The Stock Market?

The stock exchange is an organization where transactions of different financial instruments are carried out through authorized intermediaries. This institution provides the facilities for its members, brokers, or operators to negotiate the purchase and sale of securities.

The stock exchange originates from the City of Bruges, Belgium, within the Van der Burson family of bankers. These organized meetings in his palace to make commercial operations or to transact assets, and they had like shield three bags of skin. Then in 1460 in Antwerp, Belgium, the first modern stock exchange arose, for years later, expanding to other countries.

Who Integrates It?

The stock market has been made up of companies, organizations, or public and private entities, which are the applicants for capital. Savers or investors who are the capital providers and intermediaries, brokers, brokerage houses, etc. also participate.

For companies to be able to list their securities on the stock market, they must publish their financial statements to determine their financial situation. When a company makes an offer on the stock market, anyone can know the information and performance of the company.

The stock exchange works like a large market or mall where stocks are bought and sold daily. Companies are listed on the stock exchange because it allows them to obtain new capital without having to borrow or borrow.

In this medium, any company can quote, as long as it meets the standards and the minimum investment requirements.

Role of the Stock Exchange

The time has come to show you what you want so much to know. Get ready to know the aim/mission of the stock market in any part of the world:

- Facilitate the transactions of the resources so that a better allocation of them is feasible.
- Support transactions by providing legal certainty.
- Guarantee liquidity, since assets such as shares and securities are converted into money.
- Inform truthfully and permanently concerning the values, operations, financial statements of companies, among other things.
- Contribute to the growth as well as the development of the capital and securities market.
- Organize the stock market through stock market operations.

How Does The Stock Market Work?

Below I will show you how the stock market works internally.

Undoubtedly, this is information that you must know before entering this wonderful and fluctuating financial world. Do you want to know them?

When a person has to buy or sell part of a company, he does it through the stock market.

If the company sells its shares for the first time, it makes a public offering known as the "primary market."

For a company to grow, it needs additional capital that requires the contribution of new partners.

Shares are issued to find these partners that are sold in the so-called public offering to those who are interested in investing. When a public offer is made in the stock market, the company is made public, and the interested party obtains the shares.

Subsequently, this shareholder can, in turn, sell his shares in the future if he decides, according to his convenience. In the same way that other investors buy it, they also evaluate the updated information of the company for their convenience.

Analyzing the information allows the feasibility of a good offer to change significantly from one day to another.

The purchase and sale price of shares is set by free-market laws, that is, supply and demand.

Those who buy set the purchase price and those who sell do the same; this is how operations are carried out, both actors setting their stance.

The shareholder always expects to earn periodic dividend earnings, or by selling his shares at a higher price. The holder is an investor who, by acquiring a bond, expects to generate regular interest or profits at the end of the term.

Stockbrokers are responsible for conducting transactions between sellers and buyers of shares. Investments in shares are considered variable income, while investments in debt as fixed income.

Can I Invest In The Stock Market From Home?

Here I tell you everything! Investing in the stock market may seem like a complicated task and only for large entrepreneurs, but in reality, anyone can do it. I only recommend that you study very well what it is and of course you go to the experts in the stock market.

Thanks to the internet, this market can be accessed more easily from home or mobile by different applications. However, just because it is easy to invest in the stock market online does not mean that it is easy to obtain earnings by shares.

Investing in the stock market online maintains the principle of buying and selling shares; it is done through online brokers. Benefits are obtained without the need to be in a specific place to operate the exchange, from where you are.

The online brokers will be the tool that will help us gain access to financial markets to invest in the stock market. You can invest in national securities and also in any company in the world, from small to large companies.

These so-called brokers can be obtained on web pages, applications, and other means such as banks (which allow investing from home).

The procedure is generally as follows:

• Open an account in a broker, the platform for trading your preference.

• You will obtain the corresponding username and password (if applicable).

• Each account will be associated with a bank account, where the money you will use for purchase and sales orders will be. The bank account will enter the money from the sale of shares, collection of dividends, and any other operation.

• Each operation will generate its commission, and you must bear in mind the brokerage costs, administrative expenses, and stock fees.

• Brokering costs are generally based on a percentage of what is invested for the services received. The costs or administration expenses depend on the country where you open your account; the commissions vary due to different factors.

Invest in the stock market: What platform to use?

There are many platforms to invest in the stock market. Below I will mention some of the most popular brokers or online trading platforms to invest or trade.

However, don't stop to decide! Take your time to try until you get the one that makes you feel safe and comfortable according to your needs.

How much money do I have to invest in the stock market?

You may have in mind that to invest in the stock market, you need to have a lot of money, but it is not.

I have good news for you, and it is that you do not need a lot of money, although I cannot give you a specific figure. Anyone can invest in the stock market on their own, without having as much money available to start.

When you invest more money in the stock market, it does not mean higher profitability; it is recommended to think in percentage terms, in terms of investment. You should start with little money to experiment, and then increase the investment according to the results obtained.

My primary recommendation is that you should save. That is, you need to have the ability to save to generate money, which you will then invest consecutively.

It is essential to make it clear that initially, your goal should be to gain experience and train. It is a complicated world, where many people end up losing a lot of money. It occurs because they do not form before fully entering the stock market investment.

You should also take into account the impact in terms of money that the associated commissions will have on your investment. Remember the commissions for a capital increase, custody of securities, purchase, and sale, collection of dividends, etc.

Can I start investing in a stock simulator?

A stock market simulator is a computer program with a very advanced interface that allows you to learn how to spend money in the stock market online. It has all the necessary tools to practice in real-time as if you were in the stock market.

It can support you as a fundamental tool to start trading in values and make some decisions without any risk! These simulators can be found in some specialized brokers or banks, and they are complex applications that are being commonly used.

Operating a simulator can avoid many headaches, helping you to train and learn, to have good knowledge. It enables you to get familiar with the interface handling play money, seeing the results of your decisions, to jump to reality.

"Unless you can watch your stock holding decline by 50% without becoming panic-stricken, you should not be in the stock market."

– Warren Buffett

2. THE MECHANICS OF OWNING, BUYING AND SELLING STOCKS

"If you aren't thinking about owning a stock for ten years, don't even think about owning it for ten minutes."

- Warren Buffett

The use of stock shares, whether it is getting dividends or speculating on their listing, is an increasingly popular and interesting practice. Of course, the risk of loss is also present, but depending on how you buy and sell your shares, this risk may be decreased. If you are wondering how to buy and sell stocks to large companies that are listed directly online, the following explanations may interest you.

Buy Shares to Become A Shareholder

A large part of individuals and institutions that buy securities do so to become a shareholder. It is the simplest use of stocks and their main objective. Indeed, when a company issues shares, it is possible to be a buyer directly online.

However, for shares already listed, this must go through an intermediary that can be an online agent or an online bank.

Of course, it is possible to buy shares directly from sellers who bought these shares themselves in the same way that you can resell your shares.

Buy and sell stocks with online brokers

People who wish to buy and sell shares on the stock exchange can do this from their homes. They can do so through an online trading platform proposed by a Forex broker. These Forex brokers make available to investors simplified trading tools called CFDs that allow speculation in the stock market.

These CFDs or Contracts for Difference allow you to buy a batch of shares on the stock exchange at a certain price and then sell it when the price has reached a level interesting enough to give you a profit on the difference.

However, the real advantage of CFDs for buying and selling shares on the stock exchange lies in the leverage effect, which allows you to multiply your investment by 100, 200, and sometimes even 400. In this way, you can generate significant benefits when operating lots of larger stocks over a short period.

For example, if Apple shares are at € 40 and you want to buy 100 lots, in theory, you would need an investment of € 4,000. However, if you use a lever effect of 1: 200 you can buy these 100 lots for just 200 euros.

Similarly, if this share goes to € 42 and you resell the lot of 100 shares, your profit will be 100 x 2, that is, 200 euros. It means that in a few minutes, you can double your investment.

Purchase and sale orders for shares

The Forex trading platforms that allow you to buy and sell shares on the stock market also allow you to enjoy practical tools to place your orders or program them in advance.

Thus, when scheduling a sell order for a certain price level, you no longer need to follow the market live, as your positions will automatically close at the right time. This method can be used to make profits, but also to limit losses with the "stop-loss" order that triggers the sale of your shares below a certain limit.

CFDs also allow positions to be taken directly for the sale of the securities, which means betting on the drop in prices.

When is it the best time to buy shares on the stock exchange?

Buying shares on the stock exchange can be an attractive investment, but it is not about buying any stock at any time. Indeed, the purchase of shares on the stock exchange is, first of all, a decision that must be made following a strategy. But then, when is it better to buy stocks?

When it comes to equity stocks, and to create a stock portfolio, it is preferable to buy the shares of long-listed companies to know in advance the potential of each security in terms of long dividends term. You can also choose to buy the shares of the innovative companies that issue their securities for the first time to be part of their success, although this is a bit riskier.

When it comes to online trading using CFDs, buying stocks is, first and foremost, a matter of finding the right time. Indeed, from a trading platform, you can access numerous international stock securities. But be careful: you should only buy a title if you think that your price will increase over time and in a more or less long term. In this way, you can obtain benefits by reselling the most expensive shares of what you have bought them.

Therefore, we advise you to buy shares on the stock exchange under the following conditions:

- the stock follows a strong and lasting bullish trend;
- a major event has just, or is going to, influence the share's upward price;
- technical indicators announce that the trend will remain bullish or a bullish reversal of a negative trend, and
- The sector of activity from which the share comes experiences strong growth.

When is it a good idea to sell the shares on the stock exchange?

Now we will be interested in cases of sale of shares on the stock exchange. A sale can be made to recover the money to invest it again or simply to pocket the profits if the corresponding title has increased in value.

Indeed, if you own some stocks in your stock portfolio whose dividends are becoming less interesting, it would be a good option to get rid of them to add more profitable stocks. You can also sell your shares to pocket profits because they have greatly increased in value since you purchased them.

When it comes to stocks trading on an online trading platform, things get a little complicated. Of course, you can re-sell the shares you have bought, but you can also directly sell a security without ever buying it. This method consists of investing in the price of these shares.

CFDs offer the possibility of investing both in the purchase and sale of shares on the stock exchange so that every opportunity can be taken advantage of even when the market is bearish. Thus, you can sell a share when:

- its price follows a strong and lasting downward trend;
- an event will take place or has taken place, and there is a good chance that it will lead to a fall or fall in the price of this asset;
- one or more technical indicators announce a sharp decline or bearish change for a stock, and
- the sector of activity from which the corresponding action comes suffers a major economic crisis.

How long do you have to hold stocks in a short-term strategy?

If you trade short term, or even concise term, you obviously will not hold your shares too long. A strategy like Day Trading, for example, will require the resale of your lots before the end of the session.

In this specific case, it is sensible to use a crowbar effect or bet a significant part of your capital to generate a substantial profit in just a few hours. Do not set yourself too ambitious a target, as you risk not being able to achieve it in time and suffering a bearish correction before leaving the platform you are speculating on.

If you trade for several days, you will only keep your shares until you reach a realistic target of a few max points. Consider setting a stop order in the right place so that your position closes on time.

How long do you have to keep stocks in a long-term strategy?

For more long-term strategies, it is necessary to take into account the possibilities of bearish reversals in the price of your shares. These micro-movements should not force their positions to close before reaching their goal.

In effect, you will have to use stop and limit orders at the same time. The latter must be established far enough from its opening price so that its position remains open in the event of a possible correction. You should also think about having enough capital in your trading account to be able to cover these types of cases.

When should the shares be resold?

Apart from achieving the goal that you have set, some particular cases will push you to sell your shares without waiting any longer.

For example, when the price of the stocks you are following passes below a critical point indicating a strong probability of decline, it is better not to wait and close your position so as not to risk losing more money. These levels can be determined by the levels of technical support observed in the charts.

Likewise, if you follow the economic news of a company whose shares it operates, some posts may create a risk, and sometimes it is preferable to sell your shares before they expire.

What shares can be purchased or sold online?

For some years now, the offer of Forex brokers regarding CFDs for stocks has increased considerably, and now many titles can be accessed from the trading platforms we have.

Of course, you will find Spanish, European and international stocks. All the actions proposed on these platforms are part of the large international stock indices. They are, therefore, especially popular, volatile thanks to precise strategies based on technical or fundamental data.

What stocks to invest in?

As you will no doubt have observed, the actions proposed by brokers on their trading platforms are very numerous and, therefore, it is becoming increasingly difficult to choose which assets to trade.

So what stocks should you invest in? Although investing in the stock market is not an exact science and it is not possible to foresee exactly which stocks will be profitable and which will be losers, it is sensible to analyze the sectors of activity that may experience strong growth.

3. WHO IS A BROKER & HOW TO CHOOSE ONE

Do you know what a stockbroker does? What are the main functions it performs? If you are not familiar with the answer to these questions, we invite you to read the following post, in which we will clarify everything about it.

Stockbroker: What is it?

The main task of a stockbroker is to advise other people who do not have sufficient experience to carry out operations in the diverse financial markets.

The stockbroker stands out for having good knowledge of finance and playing an active and main role in the stock market. It could be said that the stockbroker acts as an intermediary. It is the person who is between the broker and the investor who is interested in buying or selling.

The stockbroker guides and advises his clients in finance so that they can obtain the best possible returns. It is also in charge of managing the purchases, and the rest of the operations carried out by its clients. So it can be said that a broker's work cycle begins when one of his clients buys an asset and ends when he sells it and definitively closes the transaction.

Stockbroker: Functions

Among the functions performed by the stockbroker, we can find:

- Intervene in the purchase/sale of assets and the management of securities.
- It is placing of new securities in the market (Public sale offer, or also known as IPO). This refers to when a company is interested in starting to go public; it should be addressed to the broker, who will be in charge of finding a buyer for its shares.
- Inform and advise the client and companies.

Characteristics of a Stockbroker

We already know before that a stockbroker is the link between supply and demand in the stock market. Now, we will see the characteristics of the stockbroker and his trade:

- It is a commercial activity that can be carried out by any type of person.
- As it is an activity that anyone can exercise, not everyone can enter to carry out stock movements and transactions, because yes, no, it must go through the acceptance of a regulator. This process requires different requirements, including A minimum age, a specific level of education on the subject, accredit such knowledge if possible.

- The broker is under strict supervision at all times, promoting the good performance of the work without malicious news.

- The stock market regulator will constantly require the financial status of your account. Likewise, you are required to maintain a stable amount of equity.

- The agent will receive a commission according to the specifications of the agreement, this varies depending on the number of operations carried out, and may receive a fixed commission on their services, without the results of the operations affecting their heading, or, you can choose remuneration according to the percentage of their results.

How to choose the right stockbroker?

Investing is not as simple as buying and selling stocks, so the help of a professional is invaluable. A proficient stockbroker will devise a plan to grow your money while keeping your goals, risk tolerance, and time horizon in mind. Unfortunately, all stockbrokers are not created equal.

There are the bad, the good, and the ugly when it comes to investing. Choose the wrong broker, and it can cost you a lot of money on investment losses and unnecessary fees.

A Background Check Is a Must

You need your broker to be licensed and registered in the state in which you reside, yet you also want to ensure you have the right credentials, enough experience. And there are no major breaches of compliance.

All of that information is available by contacting your state's securities regulator. The American Association of Securities Administrators provides a list of contact information for state regulators here.

Equally important is how the professional is paid. Stockbrokers can be paid a percentage of their invested assets, an hourly rate, a fixed rate, or a commission on the shares they sell to them.

Unlike financial advisers who have a fiduciary duty to take into account the best interests of their clients, brokers cannot earn a commission on the sale of particular stocks, bonds, or mutual funds and can earn a commission. Often it is better to turn to a feed advisor or stockbroker who does not earn a commission. Because they do not receive paid commissions, they have no incentive to drive one action or investment idea over another.

Interviewing multiple runners is a must.

A lot of thinking and searching should be done to choose a doctor, and the same diligence must be applied to finding a stockbroker. It means in addition to checking your history; You must interview multiple brokers before making a decision. It is particularly important because you want to feel comfortable with the person who handles your money.

When interviewing potential brokers, there are some key questions to ask. First, know how the broker is paid and what he can expect to pay in fees. After that, you want to know how your agent will contact you and how often.

Nothing can sour a relationship faster than an unresponsive stockbroker, especially when you're uncomfortable with an investment or when the markets are trading. Each broker will offer different investment services and products, so you also want to know what their fees are charging you. For example, does the broker offer online tools to verify your accounts, communicate, and analyze your portfolio?

Also, does the firm give you access to property research and third-party research on individual stocks, different industries, and market analysis? If you're interested in real estate or international investments, you want to make sure that the agent you go with not only offers investments in those areas but is also well-trained to invest in those industries.

Check out these red flags.

The way your agent acts during the interview can tell you a lot about that person. The goal of investing is to achieve a goal that is unique to you. At the initial meeting, your broker should ask you about your goals, risk tolerance, and time horizon. But if he or she is advocating a specific investment idea or making guarantees on return instead, you should raise red flags.

If the broker doesn't take the time to know your goals and is only interested in telling you what they can do for you, it's a telltale sign that the broker has their interest in your heart, not yours.

Do your homework with references.

Often one of the finest ways to find a good stockbroker is through word of mouth. Ask your family, friends, coworkers, and other acquaintances that they use for their investment advice, and you should be able to get a list of some names.

A referral can be invaluable, especially when it comes to someone you trust, but don't take the recommendation blindly. You need to do your due diligence, which means checking the agent's background, uncovering the fee structure, and interviewing the person to ensure their personalities identify themselves. After all, many of the investors who were scammed by Bernie Madoff and his Ponzi scheme blindly invested on the recommendation of a friend.

The Bottom Line

Investing in the stock markets can be very complex and time-consuming and often requires the help of a professional. But while a stockbroker can provide invaluable service if your money grows, not all stockbrokers are created equal.

There are the good, the bad, and the ugly. Eliminating those falls on the investor and to do that requires a bit of homework. From consulting the agent's background to asking key questions before hiring someone, there are many steps to choosing the right agent for your particular financial situation.

4. HOW TO ASSESS RISK AND VOLATILITY

Assessing risk is a step by step process and is a basic part of the risk management of an organization. However, risk management is also conducted on behalf of an individual as there are several types of risks; hence multiple ways and purposes are served to conduct a risk assessment or risk analysis. Mainly, two types of risk are undertaken in a casual way, and that includes:

Individual risk assessment

Within individual cases and transactions, the risk is always involved. Risk can be assessed and analyzed in case of interaction between a physician and patient, a teacher and a student, a buyer and seller, and so on. It means whenever individuals interact with each other for any purpose. Individual risk can happen to occur between both sides.

However, individual risk assessment is affected by several factors like behavioral, psychological, ideological, religious, and others depend on the purpose of an individual's interaction with each other. Individual risk assessment affects rationally the whole process for which individuals interact with each other, and dealings and transactions are made among people.

So, there may be several requirements for individual risk assessment just depending on the nature of the task to be done by individuals, transactions to be made between them, and interaction is done among individuals. Whatever the purpose or reason for meeting individuals with each other, risk assessment and analysis becomes necessary to run the process smoothly.

Systematic risk assessment

Systems risk assessment or management can be seen in larger scenarios and broader sense. It can also be said an organizational risk assessment process that may require multiple problems, functional issues, and safety hurdles, etc.

Well, systems can be of two types like linear and non-linear. Whatever the type of system, several types of problems may occur over there, and it becomes essential to assess and analyze risks involved in each system. Risk can involve at all scales; from nuclear technology to food safety system and organizational or systems risks is evaluated on different parameters and requirements.

So, how to assess risk is another important point of our discussion, and the process of risk assessment involves identifying the amount of risk in a system. According to statistical and mathematical parameters, there are different ways to assess risk, and some of these are used commonly, but some are not used in routine life. Commonly used measurements of risk assessment include:

Standard Deviation

Standard deviation is a commonly used method for assessing and calculating risk; it measures the dispersion of data from its expected value. This particular method of assessing risk is used in the commercial industry, where investors have to make decisions about making investments or not. The current and expected rate of return is measured and compared for important decision making in the industry.

Beta

Beta is another one important tool to measure risk value in both individual and systems risk management processes. It is a mathematical and statistical term that is used to calculate the expected and current value of risk involved in any system or individual interaction. If a system has a beta value of more than 1, it would be considered the risk involved in the stock market.

Value at risk

The level and value of risk are analyzed with the help of this mathematical tool, and it is also commonly used in measuring risk in the stock market. The maximum potential loss of an organization is judged using this value at risk method, and important business decisions are made according to the results of the assessment of risk in the industry and stock market.

Conditional Value at risk

This is another important and commonly used way to calculate and assess risk in the industry and stock market. Basically, tail risk is assessed using this tool, and it is also helpful in understanding the current condition of the stock market and other industries.

Risk management and risk assessment are categorized in two ways; systematic risk assessment and unsystematic risk assessment. Systematic risk is assessing risk about the market, and it also affects the overall security of the market.

However, systematic risk assessment is considered unpredictable, but hedging can be helpful in mitigating the risk of the industry. For example, unfair political affairs can affect a large span of industry and stock market, and this can be said a systematic risk involved in the stock market and other related industries of a country. Put options technique is used to sort out this type of risk.

Unsystematic risk is all about risk is involved in a particular organization, company, or sector. This type of risk is diversifiable, and it can be mitigated by the asset diversification process. A particular stock, company, or industry can be affected by this type of risk.

What is Volatility?

Volatility is a particular mathematical and statistical term that is used in measuring the dispersion of a security system, a company's rate of return, and the stock market index. In most business and commercial cases, if the volatility is higher, the risk is also considered higher in the particular industry.

Multiple statistical tools are used to measure volatility in the commercial sector and the stock market. Volatility represents the current value of assets of an industry, and important business decisions are made, and strategies are formulated according to the recent condition of the company's finances.

Volatility is also referred to as the amount of risk that is involved in security and other systematic approaches of an organization. If the volatility of an organization is lower, it would be considered that the security value will not fluctuate at once.

Traders, analysts, and risk managers use different techniques and tools to measure and assess volatility in the stock market index position. Often high volatility is considered a sign of high risk involved in the business sector and stock market sector.

Trade and business become riskier if the measuring parameters show high volatility in the stock market index. Volatility is measured by commonly used statistical tools like standard deviation, Beta, and variance.

Standard deviation is a common statistical tool that is used to measure market volatility, and Bollinger Bands is used by traders and investors to make decisions and formulate strategies in the stock market.

Maximum drawdown is another one important tool to assess volatility in the stock market, and it is useful in calculating the index points in the stock market as well. Stock price volatility is also measured by the drawdown method of assessing risk and volatility.

A beta is also a common tool that is used to measure the stock market volatility and also helpful in determining the diversification and benefits of other assets of the industry and stock market.

Regardless of measuring tools for assessing volatility, it is also important to discuss the types of volatility in the stock market and other market sectors. There are two major types of volatility that go hand in hand in all market sectors and the stock market, and they include:

Implied Volatility

Implied volatility is known as projected volatility, and it is used to determine metrics of the stock market and other option traders. Having implied volatility, traders and investors are able to determine the right position of industry and stock market, and they can go ahead in all of their business dealings and transactions.

In this way, traders are also able to calculate the probability of the current stock market index and related trade and industry. However, implied volatility does not work in scientific affairs; hence there is not forecasting about how the market and industry will move forward in recent conditions.

Having implied volatility, traders cannot rely on the past performance of the organization and rate of return to move on in existing market conditions. They have to make estimates about the potential of the options in the stock market.

Historical Volatility

Historical volatility is also referred to as statistical volatility, and it gauges the fluctuations of security approaches after measuring and assessing price changes over. The rise in historical volatility means the price of a security will also move to the top than its normal range.

This is the time when traders and investors expect some unusual changes in the stock market and other market sectors. If historical volatility drops down, traders are not able to move on ahead in making decisions about business development or making any investment in the industry or stock market.

Whatever the types and categories of Volatility in the stock market, it can be assessed and measured by well-known statistical tools and approaches like standard deviation, co, efficient, Beta, and making a bell-shaped curve in diagrams of measuring volatility. Investors and traders use to compare different tools of measuring and assessing volatility, and it remains helpful for them to deal with different approaches to volatility.

Volatility and risk go hand in hand in all business sectors and stock market industries. If the volatility of the stock market is high, the risk is also higher, and if volatility goes down, then there is a low risk for making investments in the stock market.

Investors and traders need to have the most reliable and valuable tools for measuring and assessing volatility and risk involved in their business industry and the stock market. And remember a tip:

"I will tell you how to become rich. Close the doors. Be fearful when others are greedy. Be greedy when others are fearful."

– Warren Buffet

5. TOP INDICATORS OF A WINNING INVESTMENT

When it comes to stocks, people are always afraid of losing their money because of the lack of the right strategy. You can make your investment secure by applying different strategies. Some people try to learn about indicators of a winning investment, which helps them to grow their business.

If you follow the indicators in the right way and wisely, they will minimize the chances of loss and can help make more profit. These indicators are helpful for both long term and short term investment. All these indicators are present on stock market websites.

Some top indicators of a winning investment in the stock market are mentioned below:

Trend line

Type

Trend indicator

Computation

When three rising price bottoms are connected, they make an uptrend, and when three falling price bottoms are connected, they make a downtrend.

Signals

When stocks are showing above an uptrend, it means that the market is positive and bullish, but when stocks show below a downtrend, it indicates that the market is negative or bearish.

Takeaway

If you are planning for the investment, but when the market goes above, then the downtrend line. If you are looking for profit or avoiding the chances of loss, then sell when market prices go below the downtrend line.

Simple Moving Average

Type

Trend indicator

Computation

A simple moving average is simply the average fluctuation of the stock market in a selected period. Investors use this method for the long term and short term investment. People who set a plan to invest for the short term calculate average fluctuation for the last ten days.

Traders who plan for long term investment calculate average fluctuations in the stock market for the last 100 or sometimes more than 200 days.

Signals

If the stocks remain above than long term indicators in which investors applied a simple average method of 100 to 200 days, then the stock market is considered to be positive and bullish.

So it makes it easy for the traders to have a sense of making the right decision to invest at the right time.

Takeaway

When stocks approach long term moving average, then this is the perfect time to make your investment in the stock market, but when prices go below then moving average, then this is a time to sell. This technique is really helpful for making your money secure in stocks.

Rate of change

Type

Momentum indicator

Computation

When we talk about stocks, we must have to pay close attention to the rates which are changing with time. Rate of change is one of the best indicators which is used to check for the percentage change in prices in the selected period. Most commonly, traders use 14 days rate of change indicator, which helps them to understand better.

What it signals

After calculation, the positive rate of change indicates than the stock market is now positive, and prices are rising. The negative rate of change means the stock market is negative or prices are falling.

Takeaway

Fluctuation in the rate of change indicates that stock prices will make possibly turnaround. When prices are rising, but the rate of change is not affected, it indicates the reverse of trend.

Relative strength Index

Type

Momentum indicator

Computation

The relative strength index is based on the average ratio of high prices when stock rates rise. It also includes the average ratio of low prices when the stock market falls. This indicates how much a price can rise and fall on average. On the graph, it is plotted between 0 and 100.

What does it indicate?

You will have all the information about the relative strength index by Paying close attention to the graph. If the graph rises above then 70 to 80 it indicates that stocks are overbought. If the graph falls below 30 to 20, it signals that stocks are oversold.

Takeaway

Set up a plan to make the investment if the relative strength index goes above than 30 to 40 twice consecutively. Sell to make a profit or avoid loss when the relative strength index goes above than 70 to 80 twice consecutively.

Moving Average Convergence Divergence

Type

Trend and momentum indicator

Computation

Convergence Divergence is a difference between twelve and twenty-six-day moving average.

What does it indicate?

If you are searching for the best way to have an idea of an upward trend and downward trend in the stock market, then moving average convergence divergence indication can help you.

If the rate of moving average convergence divergence is increasing, then this indicates an upward trend. If it is falling, it indicates a downward trend.

Takeaway

Most commonly nine days, moving average convergence divergence is considered for buying and selling stocks. Make investment when it goes above than 9-day moving average and sell when moving average convergence divergence reaches below than nine days moving average.

Bollinger Bands

Type

Fluctuation, Trend, Momentum indicator

Computation

Bollinger bands indicator is composed of three lines. The first one is 20 days moving average second one is the upper band, and the third and last one is the lower band. The two bands upper and lower are plotted in such a way that they act as two standard deviations, and their core is moving average.

What did it indicate?

If you are interested to see the trend, it is indicated by the moving average. Now the gap between these two bands, which are upper and lower, signals the fluctuations in the stocks.

Takeaway

When prices start reaching the upper band during high fluctuation in the market shows stocks are overbought. On the other hand, when prices start decreasing or falling towards the lower band due to a high rate of fluctuation, this indicates that the counter is oversold.

Fibonacci Retracements

Type

Trend indicator

Computation

Percentages 23.6%, 38.2%, and 61.8% are considered the golden ratio in the stock market, which is based on the Fibonacci number series.

What did it indicate?

Whenever a fall occurs in stocks, most often stock market retraces stock prices to an extent before it happens to the beginning of the next trend. Many investors believe that these retracements occur almost close to the Fibonacci numbers golden ratio.

Takeaway

Occurring of retracement at 23.6% indicates the strong trend of upward retracement or downward retracement. Typically retracement ends on 38.2%. If the retracement goes over than 61.8%, this is the indication that the trend is over.

All about Technical Indicators

Some technical indicators are listed below:

Trend indicators

This is one of the most advanced techniques to grab an idea of market trends such as upward trend, downward trend, and sideways trend.

Momentum Indicators

When traders want an in-depth analysis of trends, momentum indicators help them out to have a better understanding of the market. They just act as warning signals. In some cases, they might be giving the right information. It does not mean that all reduction in market momentum will lead to the trend reversal.

Volatility Indicators

Understanding of fluctuation of stocks in the stock market is a goal of every person who has invested in stocks. Volatility indicators help to understand the unpredictability of the market. It is mostly measured in standard deviation.

Volume indicators

Volume indicators play a key role in making a decision, whether it is a perfect time for making the investment or otherwise. Small traders focus on this indicator because as soon people start selling volume decreases and rates also fall, then they consider it the best time for investment.

After some time people start buying once again and rates start rising, and they consider it the best time for selling with big profits.

On-Balance Volume

On-Balance volume is the most advanced technique used by professional and experienced traders. It is a more in-depth analysis of volume indicators. The on-Balance volumes gather all the information about the volume and setup all this information on a single-line indicator.

Now, this indicator adds up the volume on up days and also subtracts the volume, which is on down days. As a result, it assists in calculating the cumulative buying and pressure of selling.

It also tells us about the trends. The escalation in prices leads to the rising of On-Balance volume. Drop down in prices leads to the falling of On-Balance volume.

Average Directional Index

After knowing trends, it is most important to learn the concept of trend strength. Usually, it is graphed on a single line with the value ranging from 0 to 100. It is the most powerful technique which helps the investors to have a better understanding of a stronger zone.

Average Directional Index helps traders to build more confidence and aggressive position.

When the values on the graph reach above 20, it indicates the rise in the average directional index, and it represents that trend is getting stronger.

Relative Rotation Graph

This is one of the unique indicators which is used to visualize trends in the relative strength of even more than one or multiple securities against each other.

This helps to indicate relative outclass performers in the market and tell you to pay attention to the specific area of the market, which deserves the most. According to the most expert people in stocks, the relative rotation graph indicator helps to build a portfolio.

Final words

Indicators are simply the warning signals that give you certain information about different things, such as trend reversals. These can be used to have a deep understanding of the stock market. Before working on any indicator and going for the live trade, you just need to gather all the information related to that specific indicator.

Each of the indicators can be used in many different ways. Also, it can provide you with more in-depth information as long as you try to research it. It may be a tricky process for beginners who are just starting or have not started yet.

6. BASIC INVESTMENT TECHNIQUES

Investing a portion of your earnings is always a smart decision, especially in a world where nothing is permanent.

You never really know when you might end up needing your investments or savings. You don't always end up in need of them, but when you do, having a backup investment plan managed properly is a great way to sum up, your lifetime earning efforts. This way, when the hard time comes, you can be sure that you didn't work hard all your life to simply end up with nothing at all.

However, when you aren't very familiar with investment techniques, and you're more of a novice in this phase, you might end up investing your earnings in something useless or a waste of money.

Now to avoid such situations as a newbie in investing your earnings, its better you go through the basic techniques. This way, you can be sure that you'll end up investing your precious savings in something that's actually worth it.

You might think of looking for sources to help you learn these basic techniques, right? Well, you don't really have to go anywhere else, as we've got you covered with just the right basic techniques you'll need to start as a beginner in this. So let's not waste any more time and just go ahead to discover some such basic techniques.

10 Basic Investment Techniques for Beginners

1. Set a Goal

When you start investing your money, you need to firstly think of what you really want from your investment. This means that even if your basic motto is to earn money through your investment.

You should mainly determine what your income is along with your financial condition, how much you can really invest according to your circumstances, and how much profit you would need.

2. Early Investment is Beneficial

Yes, it is true, whether you're a college student or studying in high school, the sooner you consider investing in something that benefits you, the more it will get easier for you to invest with time.

This simply means that your earnings would increase over time, while the investments you make would also benefit you with the passage of time. Hence, with all these aspects, starting early would help you invest less money in the future and again more of the profit.

So it doesn't matter how less you can invest in the first place or what options you've got with the least of your savings or earnings; it's all going to benefit you over time. So just go for it as early as possible!

3. Invest a Constant Figure Automatically

Often we consider stalling and storing our money for some uses and needs, whether they're important or just something we're keen to invest in. And in such situations, we often utilize our investment money in such ways, ending up with no money to invest at all.

This gives the least motivation for investing further, and sooner when you'll notice, you'd probably forget about investing at all. But since it is really important for the upcoming time of your life, its better you go for an automatic investment option.

This way, the money you set aside for investing every month would be automatically taken from your account through brokerage service firms or automated investment services. Also, with this, if you even forget about the investment money, these services would make them don't.

4. Don't Invest Too Much

Now considering investing a great amount of your savings or earnings with the idea of having it doubled or profited into a figure that would leave you overwhelmed is good – and also something we all think of.

When you do start investing anything anywhere, it's important you snap yourself out of those fantasized dreams and get realistic.

This means that you can't go with investing a great number of your earnings without keeping your basic expenses in mind. Since you aren't sure of when the profit might arrive, and these bills are more of a constant paying need.

Hence, starting small with your investments, while calculating the money you'll need for your needs is certainly a great way to manage your earnings while also investing them.

5. Do Your Homework on Investment

Yes, we all need this, quite aware of everything basic when it comes to investment. But that's certainly not enough when you're getting ahead with choosing options and managing the dealing process on your own. Since this is more of official business, and you can't just act amateur and new in this, even when you are.

Hence, studying the basic terminology on making the right decisions and furthermore on stocks, bonds, funds, CDs, and other such investment options – is really important.

This way, you won't only learn about investment options and what suites you according to your position, but you'll also learn how you should deal with your investment and make decisions according to the market efficiency.

All this homework would certainly benefit you in the beginning, as well as for future investment needs.

6. Don't Pay High Commission

Remember this, when you go to professionals to help you look for investment options that would profit you well, you might end up being scammed by these professionals. This isn't something obvious, but as a newbie, you might end up facing these situations.

Hence, to avoid it, it's important you don't blindly trust professionals who would take a high commission from you for the investment options and further process.

In this way, you might end up paying a large commission to the professionals, while being rewarded with the least of profit afterward.

Hence, before you trust any professional and their commission demands blindly, its better you study on them and research on the investment options they offer you with. This would keep you safe from any kind of loss.

7. Don't Invest in One Place/Stock

Well, investing in stocks doesn't always result in large profits, but also leads you to equal losses. However, it's in your hands if you need to limit your losses and keep it all neutral.

For this, you can always look for investment options that are completely different from what you are already investing in.

This way, when one market ends up going down for a while, the other would be up. Hence, you won't just be left with loss only, but rather both profit and loss. This would be a way of diverse investment for you, keeping you benefitted with your investment at all times.

8. Invest in Long-term Options

This is highly beneficial, and that is why some of the top investors recommend beginners and everyone looking for basic investment techniques to always invest in long-term options. This mainly means that when you consider the short-term profits offered by a company and only do timely research on it, you might not end up gaining profits with that investment option for long.

So instead, investing in what might keep you happy and pleased for the next ten years, despite the ups and downs, are certainly the right company's you should look for. Hence, when you research on any company or investment option, make sure it is based on solid fundamentals as well as a strong and consistent long-term prospect.

9. Keep an Eye on Your Portfolio

Now before you start thinking what this basic technique is mainly referring to, let's get to the point here. So keeping a specific portfolio carried in terms of your investments is very good.

However, you can't always invest in the same place and never really go for a change. Because most of the time, we find options that are much better in the profit or the previous ones just don't profit us much anymore.

Hence, keeping track of your portfolio and changing your investment options every time the economic market changes would certainly be a smart move. This way, you can stay away from the investments that are giving you loss, even when they once offered you great profit.

And also, you can explore new options from time to time and make the most out of your money through these options.

10. Continue Research

As mentioned several times earlier, learning more on the economic market and what goes on in the present time is always a smart move in terms of investment.

This means that even when you've invested your money somewhere and have learned the most of that aspect and what's trending, you don't have to stop there.

But instead of that, reading and studying about the things you've invested in while also staying intact with the market trends every now and then, along with the global economic change – all would surely help you make smarter decisions in the future.

Final Words

Investments are the smart way everyone plans to save and benefit from their income nowadays. Whether you're someone old, a young entrepreneur, or just a student, you've surely come across multiple investment options several times in your life.

As much as it all seemed pleasing, beginners find investing their money anywhere a lot frightening too. A simple reason for that is the fact that they might end up losing their precious earnings or savings.

But even if you are new in something, it shouldn't be what stops you from taking a step forward. Instead, leaning the new ways of making more profit and the tons of options you've got today to invest in; is always a great way to spend your money as well as time.

Now that you've even got some basic techniques that can help you get started and going in your investment journey just righty, there' really nothing more you should be worrying about. So without having any second thoughts, just go ahead and apply these techniques for your better future!

Pro Tip:

"Patience is the key when you are investing in the stock market."

7. WHAT YOU SHOULD KNOW ABOUT TAXES

The stock market is a great place to pour in your savings as an investment. As only with some basic skills and knowledge on this market, you can make a great profit out of it. However, that's surely not all to what it is, as there are losses too.

But that's mainly what the stock market mainly revolves around; the losses and the profits. It's never really the same, and as much as you invest in it, the more you get to have a hold on this aspect.

However, learning just about the basics of what might result in a loss and what would profit you is not the only thing one should study. As when you're a beginner, you'd probably end up in situations that would ask you to understand more than just that.

Now, this can refer to a lot when it comes to learning everything about stock markets, but what I'm mainly referring to are the taxes.

Now whether you're a newbie in the stock market or someone who was around for a while now, learning the role of tax here is essential.

As only this way, you can be sure to make better investments in the right stocks; while understanding the tax criteria according to your position. So for a clearer view on everything about tax in the stock market, let's discuss some basics below.

The Long-term Capital Gains Rate Criteria

This tax rate is mainly applied to your profit, which is less in comparison to the rate that is applied to your other income that applies a tax. As an example, if your tax rate is 15%, you're most likely to pay a tax of 5% on your stock's profit.

Whereas, if you've got a tax rate of 25% to pay, then your profits tax rate would be 15%. However, this tax rate is mainly applied to the profit kept for a year or more, which is gained by the sale of your stock.

But that's not the tax rate applied to the profit from stock selling that is kept for less than a year. As instead, when you've got profit stored for less than a year, you're more likely to pay the tax rate for it, which is equal to the ordinary tax rate you pay on your income.

Reducing Tax on your Stock Sales

Here is a point to remember, when you determine the profit of your stock sale in a specific calculation method, you are more likely to understand the exact meaning of the variables in the formula. This mainly means that you can plan the exact amount in a way that you reduce the liability of the tax when you sell your stock.

Now, most of the time, we consider the full amount of the check received after selling stock to be the one that we should pay a tax on. However, that's certainly not the complete truth, as there are ways you can subtract the amount of tax you pay according to how much you can.

A simple formula to get this done is to subtract the basis of your tax amount to the sales you've received, and you'll get a deductible loss or a taxable profit you can eliminate from this profit of yours. This way, you won't really end up losing too much of the unexpected tax from your profit, especially when you don't even want to.

Now one might consider how they can really reduce the sales proceeds in all this calculation so that you don't pay too much tax, right?

Well, a simple and obvious way to do that is to pay some commission to a broker who would help you get through this. So instead of paying too much on the tax, you can pay a little in order to make sure you can get along with this formula of reducing your sales tax.

Next, is the basis in the formula just mentioned? Well, if you're still wondering what that might refer to, and then you can consider it to be the main cost of the stock you'll be selling. However, that's not all, as it can also include the dividends that you've reinvested in the stock or the commissions you pay to the opposition.

Yet, in some cases, if you've inherited a stock, then the basis would simply be determined as the fair market value of the stock after the date of the decedent's death. Also, if you've received the stock as a gift to you from someone, then you can consider the basis to be a lower amount of the fir-market value, according to its value, at the time the gift was sent to you.

Experimenting with the Wash Rule

Now you might have heard of this rule in the stock market, but understanding it from a closer perspective is also very important. Since we're mainly discussing taxes in the stock market, this rule also revolves around just that.

However, it's mainly the practice of selling a stock for profit when you're in the position of gaining loss from it, and when you do sell it and gain the profit, you buy it back instantly.

Now, this isn't really what the rule mainly is, but rather where you can apply it in your stock affairs. Hence, with the help of the 'wash rule,' you get to prevent the loss you'd get on the sale of a stock if you buy its replacement stock in the time period of 30 days.

This mainly helps you get out of the limitations applied by the IRS; that doesn't allow an investor to claim the loss after selling stock and then buying it again in less than 30 days. Hence, when you've got the 'wash rule,' you can make less loss through a stock.

Deduction of Capital Losses

When you face losses in your stock market, you are allowed to deduct an amount with respect to the losses from your tax returning amount. Now as much as this is a benefitting factor of the stock market, you're also supposed to face some limitation here.

This means that you are only allowed to gain a specific amount of your losses through the tax return every year. Hence, no matter how many stocks you sell at a loss, you are going to be able to deduct only $3,000 per year. And the rest of your loss would be taken forward to provide to you in the coming years.

However, if you're willing to first calculate all your losses and gains through this specific limitation and understanding how what you'll be ending up with, you can always apply the capital losses against the capital gains you achieve – both in the present year and the one's coming afterward.

Other Deductible Expenses in Investment

Often we don't pay attention to a specifically less tax deduction from our profits, which is mainly the commission of the brokers in the stock market. However, these aren't just any brokers, but rather the one's who either manage our mutual fund account or simply provide us with advisory services in the stock market. And so, this tax amount is deducted as a fee for their services offered to us.

But if you don't feel like allowing the deduction of this fee, then you've always got a long-term option of having these fees deducted back to your account. This deduction to provide your fees back to you can take place as an investment expense on Schedule A, which would be possible on your tax return.

Now in terms of understanding the exact amount deducted from your profit for the broker fees, you'll need to do a little work. This doesn't mean proper research and study on it, as most of the broker fees depend upon the 1099s of year-end statements – where you can find a statement provided on the total charged fee for a year.

But since many brokers do not follow this criterion, you might simply have to contact your broker and ask them for how much fee you paid. This way, you can have a clear idea of how much you would want to take back as the deduction.

Final verdict

Almost everyone nowadays considers the stock market as a great source of investment and profit income. And so, we'd quite often notice how most of the people around us are a part of this market. And why not? When there's such a huge stock market available for you to invest and gain profit from, there's hardly any reason one should step back from it.

However, even with all the pros on might consider this hugely benefiting market, there are certainly some loopholes one should consider before stepping into it. Now one obvious one here might be the fact that you might lose just as much as you would gain (unless you don't master the investing techniques). But other than that, the tax factor in the stock market is also something one should study about; before you end up noticing that your profits have lessened.

Now keeping that in mind and the fact that not many consider the taxing of their stocks to be as important of an enlightening subject for them as others in this aspect, we've aligned everything important you should learn about. Now keeping that in mind and the fact that not many consider the taxing of their stocks to be as important of an enlightening subject for them as others in this aspect; hence, just go ahead; and make the most of it!

8. ALL ABOUT THE BULL & BEAR MARKET

Incorporate the world; you must have heard the words Bull and Bear; this is a general description for dual market conditions rise and down. Simply, a bull market is just about the market is on the rise, and its economy is sound and stable, whereas a bear market describes the down condition of the economy in which stocks are in decline in value.

This particular name and the term is used to describe what markets are doing in general and what its positions in the current situation are. Bull and Bear also narrate about appreciation and depreciation of market value. Investors and traders are also given names as Bullish and Bearish according to the particular market conditions.

Bull and Bear both names are just phrases that indicate the current condition and situation of the market; hence behavior and mentality of investors and traders can also be judged in a particular scenario. If the market is Bull, the investors would be named as Bullish, but if the market is bear, then they would be called Bearish.

There is a historical background behind these particular terms and names of market conditions, and they are related to the psychology and gestures of both animals bear and bull. However, it is also said that actual expression for these terms is just unclear right now, but it can be described according to bull and bear's action.

For example, a bull is always seen to attack by its horns upwards while the bear is analyzed attacking swap its paws downwards. So these factors can be considered for giving names to market conditions; up and down.

Actions of both animals are related metaphorically to the market conditions. If the economy is up, it would be considered a bull market, and if the stock goes down, it would be named as a bear market.

Whatever the origin of these phrases and terms, they are interesting and seen to be rational in the corporate world. Our next discussion would be based on all about the bull and bear market. What market conditions and indicators can fall in both types of terms or categories? So, keep reading the following lines for the interesting narration of the bull and bear market.

Some of the usual indicators of the bull market include:

High Gross Domestic Products

This is simply a usual indicator for a well-established, stable, sound, and flourishes economy as it is bull market condition. In this particular condition, GDP remains high; hence consumer spending is also upward.

Rising Stock Prices

Rising stock prices leave a very good impact on the mentality and behavior of people associated with bull market conditions, and they get more confident in making investments in the industry. Prices and rates are also increased in this particular market condition.

Longer Stock Trading

The whole environment and climate of the market last cool and hopeful, so investors feel free to busy their shares on more business sides. This is the reason this condition is related to longer stock trading terms.

Lower Unemployment Rates

In bull market conditions, more and more people are hired on jobs, and there is no concept of unemployment. Up-gradation of business means there is growth in the workforce, and most of the people are hoping to be part of the good ear of industry.

Another good point of bull market conditions is that it remains longer than bear market conditions. Not only this, but the average total return for a bull market is also seen to grow. If we see a global scenario of bull market conditions, we can find notable examples of bull market conditions in the corporate world historically. Like:

The Bull Market History

The 1940s-1950s

It was a time after post second world war, and it was the bull market condition when the US economy was at the top, and most of the soldiers were returned to their homes.

1980s-2000s

This was also a golden period for US economic conditions, and it was a bull market when a 600% average return rate was determined to be gain in the overall corporate world.

Today

US economic conditions have consistently grown up since 2017. This is also said to be a golden era of the corporate world in the United States as jobs are always available over there, average returns for investment have grown up, investors are always ready to put their part in trading activities and business.

So this is a bull market in a nutshell; however, whatever the condition of the bull market is, it can exist with a bear market. Further, we are going to describe the same information about the bear market. So don't leave it without reading the following lines.

In contrast with the bull market, a bear market is just all about going down, getting pessimism, the condition of trade is stagnation, trends are down, people are unconfident and insecure, stocks are sold rather than buying, etc. This is a bear market condition where there are no jobs, no hope, no business planning at all.

The Bear Market Indicators

Some of the usual indicators for the bear market include:

Fall down of Market Prices

Investors and traders become bearish in a bear market, and they are not willing to buy a new share of the business that results in complete fall down in market prices and stability of industry as well.

Complete Unemployment

Unavailability of jobs or relatively low rates of employment is a clear sign of bear market. Fall down of companies and shareholders results in layoffs and downfall of the workforce as well.

Shorter Stock Trading

In the bear market, stock trading conditions get more bearish, and investors do not buy and sell stock shares. The industry stops at all.

Although a bear market is seen to be very bad, it does not last long at all. A study by Morningstar reveals the fact that average bear market conditions last just for 1.4 years in the history of the corporate world.

Regardless of indicators and facts about the bear market, there are several notable examples of the bear market that last in the history of the US economy.

The Bear Market History

1929s

During this session of the year, the US economy was seen to be paralyzed entirely as there were no jobs; people get homeless and lost wellbeing. Not only America but the entire world was impacted by the bear market conditions in the United States in 1929.

The 2000s

This was the time when there was a severe downfall of tech companies in the United States, and it was called a bear market.

2008s

2008 was the time for the housing market crash. This was a severe bear market as there were no jobs, homeowners lost their homes and traders get empty and fail to even think about investing in stock shares. This bad bear market is felt till now the United States has come into the bull market.

Investors and traders are always seen scary about the bear market as it is a scary and empty region in the corporate world, but it does not last long as we have seen in the previous history of the United States economic survey and information.

From our discussion put above, you can now better understand a clear difference between the Bull and Bear markets. Both conditions are contrary but go hand in hand with each other.

You know, up and downs are parts of life, and everyone has to go through both of these phases, whether it relates to the personal life of an individual or it is associated with a corporate world. We can say that the Bull and Bear market reflects the general overview and behavior of practical life.

Don't you think that this particular term or name of market conditions is pretty much interesting? These market conditions are associated with the attack actions of two animals Bull and Bear.

Well, the importance and existence of both the Bull and Bear market are undeniable, but both animals are remarkable for their incredible and unpredictable strength to attack and defense. Some facts reveal the evidence of Bull and Bear market concepts from the era of Elizabeth and ancient times when bull and bear were together to entertain the people come in the crowd.

The fight between Bull and Bear is famous in this regard, and this is the reason both market conditions are named accordingly.

So, what do bull and bear market means for you become important to ask after giving you solid facts and information about bull and bear market? Hopefully, this would be pretty much enough about the bull and bear market. Good Luck with your investment!

9. COMMON STOCK EXCHANGE TERMS AND WHAT THEY MEAN

If you are planning to start investing your money in the stock market, then there are some common stock exchange terms that you must know. These terms are very important in understanding the behavior of the stock market.

You should also have known the basics before diving onto the live trade. If you want to become a successful trader, these terms will assist you in achieving your goals and building your career in the stock market.

What is the Stock Market?

In short, any exchange allows people to buy and selling of stocks and give permission to companies to issue stocks to people. Stocks represent the company's ownership or equity. Shares are the units of the company. When people invest in the stock market, it means that they have bought shares of one or more than one stock.

What does the stock exchange term mean?

Stock exchange terms are slang specifically for industry security. Professionals and expert traders use these terms to talk about different game plans, patterns, charts, and many other related elements of the stock market industry.

Common stock exchange terms are listed below:

1-Annual Report

The annual report is specifically made by the company for its shareholders. This report is designed in such a way that it attracts the shareholders. The annual report carries all the information about the company's shares and their game plan for the present and future. When you are going through the annual report, you are gathering information about the company's financial situation.

2- Arbitrage

This is one of the most advanced terms in the stock market, which every trader should know. This refers to buying stocks at a low price from one market and selling at a higher rate on another market.

For example, sometimes a stock ABC trade on 50$ on one market and the same stock on the other market trade on 55$ so traders buy shares on low price points and sell them on higher rates to make the profit.

3-Averaging Down

When stock prices fall, and you plan to buy stocks on lower rates, your average buying prices decrease. This strategy is used most commonly in the stock market. After buying, you plan to sell those stocks shares when the stock market rebounds.

4- Bear Market

A bear market is opposite to Bull market. It means that the overall market is negative or falling. In this stage, the market falls up to 20% the quarter after quarter. This is one of the scariest situations for big investors because their investments are at great risk.

5- Bull Market

Bull Market is opposite to the bear market. Bull market meant the rising of the stock points. In this stage, people start investing money in the stock market because of their positive behavior.

6- Beta

This is the whole relationship between the stocks and the overall market. If stock ABC has a beta of 5.5, it means that for every one-point movement in the market, the stock ABC moves 5.5 points and vice versa.

7- Blue Chip Stocks

These are the stocks that large backup companies and leading industries. Blue-chip stocks are well known for their management and sound records. This expression is thought to be derived from casinos where blue gambling chips are used.

8- Bourse

In short, Bourse is a modern and more advanced name of the stock market. It means where people gather for the purchasing and selling of stock shares. Most commonly, it refers to Parris stock exchanges or non-US stock exchanges.

9- Broker

Many people who are beginners and don't understand the behavior of the stock market make contact with different brokers. These brokers are experienced traders who have sound knowledge of trading of stocks. These beginners contact these brokers and ask them to buy and sell stocks for them. Brokers charge high commissions for these services.

10- Bid

Bidding is as common and simple as we do in freelancing and other daily projects. In stock market bidder, who is a buyer bid for a specific share. Bid means the buyer willing to buy the share on his desired rates. The bid is made according to the asking price of the seller.

11- Close

Simply this refers to the time when trading will stop, and the stock market will close. Its timings vary from country to country. Each stock market has its own time of closing and opening. After closing the stock market, it is not available for live trade.

12- Day trading

This is one of the most advanced terms in the stock market. Day trading refers to buying and selling of stocks shares on the same day. This method is used by many experienced traders.

After buying shares, people wait for the next day to sell them at much higher rates. But there are 50/50 chances that they may end up with profit or loss. So, Day trading is a smart strategy, but it requires a lot of experience to make profits.

13- Dividend

Many companies offer incentives to attract more traders to their company. Some companies pay their shareholders one of their earnings portions, which are called the dividend. Some companies pay dividends annually or quarterly. Not all companies offer a dividend.

14- Exchange

Exchange refers to a place where thousands of investments are traded daily. There are many popular exchanges in the world. New York Stock Exchange is one of the most popular exchanges in the world, which is present in the United States of America.

15- Execution

We are familiar with this term in the sense of computer where it means the completion of a task. In the stock market, it also acts the same as in the said case. When a trader buys or sells stock shares, after completion, it is said that the transaction has been executed.

16- Haircut

The haircut is the most known term used in the stock market. It is the slight difference between the bid made by the buyer and the asking price of the seller.

17- High

High indicates the milestone reached by the stocks. It points out that the specific stock has never reached such a high price before. In the stock market, there is also one other high. This high is used to demonstrate the milestone reached by stocks in a specific period. It may be fortnightly or in 30 days.

18- Initial Public Offering

Initial Public Offering means that when a company decides to expand its business and offers its stocks available for the public. The Securities Exchange Commissions is responsible for issuing Initial Public offering and is very strict against its rules.

19- Leverage

Leverage is considered the riskiest and dangerous game tom plays in the stock market. After having your complete research, you decide to borrow shares from your broker and set up a plan to sell them on higher rates. If you successfully sell those shares on higher rates, you again return those borrowed shares to the broker and keep the difference.

20- Low

Low is opposite to high. It indicates that the specific stocks have never fallen to this price before. Low is also demonstrated for a specific period may be weekly or monthly.

21- Margin

Margin is almost the same as that of leverage. It is also considered one of the riskiest game. It is an account that allows you to borrow money from the broker to invest that money into the stocks. Now the difference between the loan which you borrowed from the broker and rates of the securities is called margin.

Margin is not for beginners; even the most experienced traders fail to apply this strategy.

22- Moving Average

Moving average is the average price of the stock shares at a specific time. 50 and 200 are considered the best common time frames to study the behavior of the moving average.

23- Open

Simply open refers to the time when the stock market is open for the live trade. Traders start buying and selling of stocks according to their plans. This varies from country to country. Every stock market has its own time to open and close.

24- Order

Order is the same as bid, but in the order, you decide to buy or sell stock shares according to your plan after deciding your order to sell or buy the stocks. For example, if you are willing to buy 200 shares, then you have to make an order.

25- pink sheet stocks

Many beginners take start with pink sheet stocks. If you are just planning to invest in this stock market, you most probably have listened to pink sheet stocks. These are penny stocks and are traded on a small scale, and each share price is 5$ or even less than that. Because these are the shares of smaller company's, you will not find them on the big markets such New York Stock Exchange.

26- Sector

There are dozens of companies that belong to the same industry. These companies are available publically on the stock market to buy their shares. These stocks groups which belong to the same industry are called sectors.

Many experienced traders trades in a single sector, such as cement or steel. There are many advantages to investing in the same sector because it is much easy to predict the fluctuations.

10. TIPS AND TRICKS FOR INVESTING IN THE STOCK EXCHANGE

Almost everyone is searching for a shortcut, which leads them to success. Its human nature, we always look for miracles that can change everything. When it comes to the stock market, people are scared of losing their investments. They find ways that could become beneficial for them to secure their investments and make a profit.

Avoiding loss in stocks is not an easy task, and even sometimes, experienced traders fail to achieve their goals. With time by learning more and more about stock market behavior is the only way to get success.

There are some pro tips and tricks for investing in stock exchange which every trader should know:

1- Invest in Index Fund

One of the most important tips for investing is to invest in an index fund instead of looking to invest in individual stocks. It also depends upon your goals, but investing in individual funds is not a good approach.

If you are taking stocks on a serious note, then investing in an index fund in a specific sector can be a great way to build your portfolio. It also helps to focus on one thing. There are some important points to remember while investing in an index fund. These are expense ratio and assets in total.

2- Focus on Mutual Funds

It is a well-known saying that putting all eggs in one basket is always the worst choice. When you are planning to buy some stocks shares, do remember not to invest in single stocks. Always find good growth mutual funds and put your money in it. This approach is the most secure one, but it seems boring and time taking. But many people love to focus on mutual funds. This technique helps to minimize the chances of losing investment.

3- Timing the Market

Many beginners think that there are sometimes when the selling or buying of stocks can make them profits. They all end up losing their money. Learning market volatility is not an easy task. Some experienced traders also believe that timing the market is not a good way to dominate in the stock market. You have to experience about market fluctuations and sell or buy stocks accordingly. There is no best and worst time to buy or sell stock shares.

4- Set Goals

Setting up goals is always the best method that every person should follow, which leads to success. People without goals are like blind people. Before diving into the stock market, first of all, you should set the goals of your investments. When you have set a long term plan, then you will have a better understanding of what to do and how to reach the destination.

5- Five Golden steps of trading to learn:

- **Setup:** A setup is composed of a high probability pattern to follow on the chart. It also ensures the reason why you are considering a trade. You need to track them to make sure that how consistent they are.

- **Strategy:** There must be a way to trade the setup and the perfect plan for it, which seems to be working. Beginners should always work on the strategies and spend time on it.

- **Entry:** Entry can make a big difference. If you enter the right way, then you will end up making a profit. On the other hand, the wrong entry will lead you to make run out of money.

- **Stop:** There should always be a stopping point when you are going through live trade. This whole thing should be pre-planned, and you should know why you are going to stop.

- **Profit Target:** When things start getting right in your favor, you sometimes make bad decisions. Instead of regretting later on, make decisions to set a profit target.

6- Have a balance of investments

There are three types of investments, which are low, high, and moderate risk investments. All these investments have some pros and cons. keeping a balance between these three risky investments can be a wise approach. If you are just starting, then prefer to invest in low-risk investments.

As soon as you get some experience, move to the moderate and then high-risk investments. Low-risk investments can make you small profits, but instead of losing all of your money in high-risk investments, consider low and moderate risk investments.

7- Think for long term

We always look for short term methods which can make big profits. But in reality, these things are nothing. So always plan for the long term. Try to invest your time in learning the behavior of the stocks to make more profits in the long run.

8- Buy value stocks

Value stocks mean stocks that are established with minimum variations. If you want to get success in the stock market, you need to learn the volatility of the stocks. Buying value stocks can make your investments much safer and secure. While looking for value stocks, consider their earning ration and price to sales ratio.

9- Diversify investments among sectors

No one can predict the stock market uncertainty. A sudden change in the country or even abroad can affect the stock market. This sudden change may be a political activity, a storm, a disaster, or any unusual thing. Diversification of investments among sectors is a proven way to minimize the chances of losing investments.

10- How much risk you can take?

Before start trading, you should make your mind clear that how much risk you can take. There are some pros and cons of this strategy. This strategy helps to have a better understanding of your game plan. Whether you are going for long term or you have made your plan for the long term in both cases, you need to be clear about how much risk you can bear.

11- Control your emotions

One of the key activities to achieve your goals in the stock market is to be patient. The stock market is considered one of the most uncertain market. No one knows what will happen in the next minute. People lose millions in seconds.

To control your emotions at that time is a hard task. But to become a mature trader, you must have the capability to see your pockets running out of money. With a relaxed mind, you can set a plan B and C to get things in the right direction.

12- 360 Degree View

Experienced traders always dive deep into learning more about stocks every day. This is the reason because of which you gain more and more experience. Whether you are buying or selling stocks shares, you always be completely aware of what you are doing.

You must be clear about what its outcomes will be. There must be some strategies for the sudden uncertainty to keep you stable in the market.

13- Automate stocks

Automating your stocks is a key activity to gain more experience in the stock market. It also helps to build your security and play on the safe side. If you are not willing to do it manually, then Robo-Advisors are always there to assist you. When you have a habit of regular investments, then you also avoid timing the market strategy.

14- Say no to leverage

Leverage simply refers to start investing in stocks by borrowing money. There are many ways to borrow money. For example, you can also borrow from brokerage firms. Some people who are new to the stock market use this method to start their stock market journey. There are bright chances of their failure because of high risks are involved. This strategy can do work for you when you have gained much experience in stocks.

15- Choose one sector

Investing in one sector can be a better approach. Professional traders always invest in one sector. There are many advantages to investing in one sector. If your focus is on one industry, you will learn more in a short time. You will also start getting familiar with the fluctuations in the industry.

16- Risk vs. Return

Simply, more risky investments always have chances of big profits. On the other hand, less risky investments have small profit margins. So, you have to be clear with your game plan that how much return; you are willing to have. People always make foolish mistakes and goes for high-profit margins and lose their money. So instead of regretting at that time, invest in between high and low-risk investments.

17- Buy low sell higher

This is the most well-known method which almost all the traders apply. But some people get wrong with this strategy, and instead of making a profit, they end up with the loss. One of the most important factors to consider while buying low price stocks is to calculate their standard deviation.

If the stocks in which you are interested in buying to have a 15% standard deviation, you are good to go. It will be a better strategy if your stock standard deviation falls below then 15% in a short period. There are bright chances of that specific stock that now it will go up.

Final Word

Many people believe that stocks are a scam, but if you set up things in the right direction, then these stocks can make you more profit than any other business in the world. All you need is not to focus on investing your money in the stock market, but you need to invest your time to learn the stock market. No one can ever predict with 100% surety about the stocks.

But by gaining more experience, you can understand the behavior of stocks and learn about the fluctuations. Before going for the live trade, considers all the above-mentioned tips and tricks for investing in the stock market to make your journey in stocks successful.

CONCLUSION

Thank you for downloading my book on stock market investment. It is a self-help book for newbies who want to start as investors and make money. Filled with top rules, regulations, important terms, and strategies that one should know before jumping into the investment game, the book encompasses all the beneficial information needed for new investors.

Here is one question for you, may I ask? What did you learn from this book? Can you recall?

Here is what I tell everyone to remember while investing in the stock exchange:

"Rule number one: Don't lose money. Rule number two: Don't forget rule number one."

Warren Buffett

How can you make this sure? Follow the set of advice, suggestions, and guidelines given in this book. Hope you found it helpful and worthy to keep. Please do not forget to give us your feedback so we can improve further.

Thank you, Happy Investing!

www.ingramcontent.com/pod-product-compliance
Lightning Source LLC
Chambersburg PA
CBHW051538240526
45465CB00027B/607